THE 80TH BIRTHDAY TRIVIA CHALLENGE

Take A Walk Down Memory Lane With Fun Brain-Teasers And Quizzes For Eighty-Year-Olds

CHARLIE MILLER

ISBN: 978-1-64845-120-1

CONTENTS

INTRODUCTION

HAPPY BIRTHDAY!

So, it looks like you have just turned 80 - or perhaps, you're just about to… Where does the time go? One minute you're just finishing school and entering the world of work, and the next you're an octogenarian!

You might well be thinking, looking back, that a lot of this has gone by in the blink of an eye. But I would not be too sure about that. In fact, quite a lot has happened in the past eight decades or so that made a big impression - and this fun birthday quiz book is here to see how much of it you can remember!

This is your 80TH BIRTHDAY TRIVIA CHALLENGE. Inside here are 15 fiendish trivia quizzes, specially compiled to test your knowledge and your memory of the last eight decades or so. From history and politics to high school, gadgets, and classic television shows, the hundreds of questions included here will hopefully have you racking your brains for the answer - while giving you a fun walk down memory lane at the same time!

Along the way, there is lots more to keep you entertained here too, with fun facts, jokes, and bonus questions scattered throughout the book. Don't worry if you don't know the answers to any of the questions, of course - all the solutions (with some much-needed context and explanations wherever you might need them!) are listed after each quiz.

So, shall we get started with our first game? Cast your mind back to the incredibly early years, and let's see how much you can remember about the 1940s and 50s…

ROUND 1

THE 1940S AND 50S

Let's start at the very beginning… How much can you remember about the people, places, events, and sights and sounds of your childhood years in the 40s and 50s?

1. Who starred opposite Humphrey Bogart as the femme fatale Vivian Rutledge in the 1946 movie *The Big Sleep*?
    a. Katharine Hepburn
    b. Rita Hayworth
    c. Lauren Bacall
    d. Ingrid Bergman
2. Which famous figure of the 1940s and 50s made his own signature corncob pipes?
    a. Harry Truman
    b. Douglas MacArthur
    c. George Patton
    d. Winston Churchill

3. When Billboard began compiling charts of America's best-selling singles way back in 1940, Tommy Dorsey was the first person to hit Number 1 with "I'll Never…" what?

   a. "…Leave You"
   b. "…Love Another"
   c. "…Dance Alone"
   d. "…Smile Again"

4. And after 12 weeks at the top of the Billboard charts, who replaced Tommy Dorsey at Number 1 on October 19, 1940?

   a. Glenn Miller
   b. Bing Crosby
   c. Perry Como
   d. Frank Sinatra

5. These four Disney animations were released in the 1940s and 50s. Can you place them in the correct order, beginning with the earliest?

   a. *Cinderella*

b. *Pinocchio*
c. *Sleeping Beauty*
d. *Song of the South*

6. In what year of this period did North Korea invade South Korea, kickstarting the three-year Korean War?

   a. 1948
   b. 1950
   c. 1953
   d. 1955

7. What long-running CBS variety show, which ran for more than 1,000 episodes until the early 1970s, was first broadcast on June 20, 1948?

   a. *The Ed Sullivan Show*
   b. *The Muppet Show*
   c. *The Tonight Show*
   d. *The Mary Tyler Moore Show*

8. What popular musical opened on Broadway in 1956?

a. *My Fair Lady*
b. *Oliver!*
c. *Oklahoma*
d. *The Sound of Music*

9. True or False? Franklin D Roosevelt, whose presidency ended in 1945, is the only president in history to have served more than two terms.

10. Alaska and Hawaii joined the United States in the 1950s. But in what year?

a. 1952
b. 1954
c. 1956
d. 1959

11. In 1956, Guy Burgess resurfaced in the Soviet Union after going missing five years earlier. What was he known as at the time?

a. A spy
b. A cosmonaut
c. A politician

d. An artist

12. In what 1956 movie did Elvis Presley make his acting debut?

    a. *Blue Hawaii*
    b. *GI Blues*
    c. *Love Me Tender*
    d. *Jailhouse Rock*

13. The world's first nuclear-powered submarine was launched in 1954 and became the first submarine vessel to complete a submerged voyage under the North Pole in 1958. What was its name?

    a. *Nautilus*
    b. *Argo*
    c. *Constitution*
    d. *Arizona*

14. Who am I?

    I am a famous American architect and designer, born in Wisconsin in 1867. After opening a design practice in Chicago in

1893, I quickly became one of the early 20th century's most notable architects, known for my unique "Usonian" style and for establishing the Prairie School of Architecture.

I designed more than a thousand civic buildings in my career, including my famous estate, Taliesin, back home in Spring Green, Wisconsin, with my wife Olgivanna. I died in 1959 at the age of 91.

15. What position in US public life was held by Sam Rayburn from 1955 to 1961?

    a. Vice-President
    b. Speaker of the House of Representatives
    c. Chief Justice
    d. Mayor of New York

SOLUTIONS

1. C. Lauren Bacall.
2. B. Douglas MacArthur.
3. D. "…Smile Again."
4. B. Bing Crosby. Bing's hit "Only Forever" remained at Number 1 for the next nine weeks.
5. The correct order is B. *Pinocchio* (1940), D. *Song of the South* (1946), A. *Cinderella* (1950), C. *Sleeping Beauty* (1959).
6. B. 1950.
7. A. *The Ed Sullivan Show.*
8. A. *My Fair Lady*. The production starred stars Rex Harrison, Julie Andrews, and Stanley Holloway. It became one of Broadway's biggest successes and went on to gross more than $10 million by 1959.

9. True. The 22nd Amendment, ratified in 1951, limited presidents to two terms only; FDR was the first and only president prior to the amendment to win a third, and eventually fourth, consecutive term in office.
10. D. 1959. Alaska was formally admitted into the Union on January 3, 1959, and Hawaii followed on August 21.
11. A. A spy.
12. C. *Love Me Tender*.
13. A. *Nautilus*.
14. Frank Lloyd Wright.
15. B. Speaker of the House of Representatives.

DID YOU KNOW?

- Before it transferred to Broadway, *My Fair Lady* had its first preview at a theatre in New Haven, Connecticut. On opening night, Rex Harrison got such bad stage fright that he locked himself in his dressing room and refused to go on. He only unlocked the door with less than an hour before curtain went up!
- General MacArthur once had such a heated argument with President Truman that he left the Oval Office and threw up on the steps of the White House!
- The carvings on Mount Rushmore were completed in 1941. They had taken 14 years to finish!
- President Roosevelt was the first US President in history ever to have flown in an airplane. He flew to Chicago to accept the

Democratic nomination for president in 1932.

- The first person to break the sound barrier - flying ace Charles "Chuck" Yeager - did so in 1947 in the rocket-powered Bell XS-1 craft. The extraordinary feat almost did not happen, however: two days before the flight, Yeager fell from his horse and broke two ribs. Fearing the injury would have him removed from the project, he only told his wife and his best friend about the accident. Despite being in intense pain, he turned up on the day of the test flight as if nothing had happened!

Why was blackjack harder to play in the 50s?

– Because everyone wanted to twist!

ROUND 2

80 YEARS OF THE MOVIES

Cinema really came into its own in the 1940s and 50s, and as the decades have gone by, Hollywood has given us countless movie memories and on-screen moments to remember.

Let's dim the lights, then, because all the questions in this round are about films from the past eight decades or so…

1. One of the biggest hits of the 1940s was *Duel in* … what?

   a. …*The Sun*
   b. …*The Night*
   c. …*The Rain*
   d. …*The Snow*

2. Something strange happened at the 1947 Oscars. What was it?

   a. A streaker
   b. Someone was awarded two Oscars for the same role

c. There was a tie
d. There was no Best Picture award

3. Who played the title role in the 1963 epic *Cleopatra*?

   a. Vivien Leigh
   b. Deborah Kerr
   c. Elizabeth Taylor
   d. Maggie Smith

4. Which legendary moviemaker made his directorial debut with *The Maltese Falcon* in 1941?

   a. John Huston
   b. George Cukor
   c. Frank Capra
   d. Otto Preminger

5. Can you place these Best Picture Oscar winners in order, from earliest to most recent?

   a. *Ben-Hur*
   b. *The French Connection*

c. *Lawrence of Arabia*

d. *All About Eve*

6. Who am I?

I am an English actor who was born in 1907. I made my movie debut in *Too Many Crooks* in 1930, but it was not until 1939's *Wuthering Heights* - in which I played Heathcliff - that I made the move to Hollywood.

Over the decades that followed, I became one of cinema's most respected actors and prolific actors, winning four Oscars for my work both in front of and behind the camera - including a special award for my 1944 production of Shakespeare's *Henry V*.

I was knighted, given a peerage by the British state, and the Order of Merit. I was married three times, including to Vivien Leigh from 1940-1960. I died in 1989.

Today, I am commemorated in the name of London's main theatrical awards.

7. What classic 1946 movie is set in Bedford Falls, New York?

    a. *Vertigo*
    b. *Welcome Stranger*
    c. *It's A Wonderful Life*
    d. *Cheaper by the Dozen*

8. Who played Bonnie and Clyde in the 1967 movie? Score a point for each name.

9. What kind of creature is Flower in Disney's *Bambi*?

    a. Skunk
    b. Racoon
    c. Rabbit
    d. Deer

10. What classic 1975 movie was based on a novel by Peter Benchley?

    a. *The Exorcist*

b. *Marathon Man*
c. *Jaws*
d. *Duel*

11. True or False? Walt Disney is the most Oscar-nominated person in Academy Awards history.

12. In what aspect of movie making is Edith Head a famous name?

    a. Directing
    b. Costume design
    c. Music
    d. Editing

13. Who connects the movies *The Birds, Fried Green Tomatoes, Cocoon,* and *Driving Miss Daisy*?

    a. Jessica Lange
    b. Janet Gaynor
    c. Glenda Jackson
    d. Jessica Tandy

14. Studio Ghibli, Pixar, and DreamWorks are movie studios associated with what kind of film?

    a. Animation
    b. Horror
    c. Musical
    d. Documentary

15. There were 72 Best Picture Oscar winners in the 20th century, from 1927-1999. Name FIVE of them that had one-word titles.

SOLUTIONS

1. A. ...*The Sun*. Produced by legendary movie mogul David Selznick, the movie took more than $20 million at the 1946 box office (equivalent to more than $300 million today). The movie's budget was so great - and Selznick oversaw such a huge advertising and promotion drive - that in the end it only just broke even!
2. B. Someone was awarded two Oscars for the same role. Disabled military veteran Harold Russell was given an honorary Academy Award for his performance in *The Best Years of Our Lives*. But Russell, who had lost both his hands in a military accident, was also nominated in the Best Supporting category for his performance. Despite being widely expected to lose to Claude Rains (in Alfred Hitchcock's *Notorious*) as he was not a trained actor and this was his first and only

movie role, in the end Russel won the Academy Award too, becoming the first person in history to take home two Oscars for the same role!

3. C. Elizabeth Taylor.
4. A. John Huston.
5. D. *All About Eve* (1950), A. *Ben-Hur* (1959), C. *Lawrence of Arabia* (1962), B. *The French Connection* (1971).
6. Laurence Olivier.
7. C. *It's A Wonderful Life*.
8. Warren Beatty and Faye Dunaway.
9. A. Skunk.
10. C. *Jaws*.
11. True. Disney was nominated for a staggering 59 awards in his career, winning a total of 22.
12. B. Costume design.

13. D. Jessica Tandy

14. A. Animation. Studio Ghibli is the famous Japanese studio co-founded by Hayao Miyazaki.

15. Take your pick from *Wings* (1928), *Cimarron* (1931), *Rebecca* (1940), *Casablanca* (1943), *Hamlet* (1948), *Marty* (1955), *Gigi* (1958), *Oliver!* (1968), *Patton* (1970), *Rocky* (1976), *Gandhi* (1982), *Amadeus* (1984), *Platoon* (1986), *Unforgiven* (1992), *Braveheart* (1995), and *Titanic* (1997).

DID YOU KNOW?

- For including the closing line "Frankly, my dear, I don't give a damn," *Gone With the Wind* producer David O Selznick was due to be fined $5,000 (equivalent to more than $100k today!) for violating the Motion Picture Production Code with a swear word. Just weeks before the film's release, however, the Code was changed to allow both "damn" and "hell" in movies, so long as their use is not "intrinsically objectionable."
- Elvis Presley turned down the lead role in *West Side Story*.
- The actors who played the munchkins in *The Wizard of Oz* were paid less than half the salary of Toto the dog.
- Although the role eventually went to Audrey Hepburn, *Breakfast at Tiffany's* author Truman Capote had originally

wanted Marilyn Monroe to star. He later famously blamed the studio for "double-crossing" him in casting Hepburn, but it was actually Monroe who had turned down the role to star instead in *The Misfits.*

- *Some Like It Hot* was originally banned in Kansas because of the theme of cross-dressing!

What did Elvis Presley do at the hardware store?

– Returned a sander!

ROUND 3

ON THE RADIO: CLASSIC POP AND ROCK

Music styles have changed over the past 80 years, of course, but there is nothing quite like a golden oldie!

This round will take things back to where it all began, with a set of questions dedicated to classic rock and pop tracks from the 1940s, 50s, 60s, 70s, and 80s.

1. Elvis Presley's "Hound Dog" was originally released as the B-side to which of his other hits in 1956?

    a. "Don't Be Cruel"
    b. "Heartbreak Hotel"
    c. "All Shook Up"
    d. "Treat Me Nice"

2. True or False?

Despite being one of the world's biggest music stars, Bruce Springsteen has only ever had one Billboard Number 1 single.

3. Who had hits in the 1960s with "What Becomes of the Brokenhearted" and "Hold On (To My Love)"?

   a. Bobby Hepp
   b. Jimmy Ruffin
   c. Lou Christie
   d. Lee Dorsey

4. All four of these tracks hit Number 1 on the Billboard Hot 100. Can you put them in the correct order, from earliest to latest?

   a. "Save the Best for Last"
   b. "Walk Like a Man"
   c. "Say You, Say Me"
   d. "The Way We Were"

5. How many tears did classic rock band Question Mark? and the Mysterians sing about in 1966?

a. 26
b. 46
c. 79
d. 96

6. In what year did The Platters release the classic doo-wop track "Only You (And You Alone)"?

   a. 1946
   b. 1956
   c. 1966
   d. 1976

7. Whose hits include covers of "The Power of Love" and "All By Myself"?

   a. Tina Turner
   b. Aretha Franklin
   c. Annie Lennox
   d. Celine Dion

8. Who sang the theme tune to the classic 1963 James Bond movie *From Russia with Love*?

   a. Tom Jones

b. Shirley Bassey
c. Matt Monro
d. Gladys Knight

9. Who made history in 1982 when they had nine albums simultaneously on the Billboard Top Country Albums chart?

    a. Reba McEntire
    b. Hank Williams Jr.
    c. Garth Brooks
    d. Billy Ray Cyrus

10. What classic Motown act was founded in 1953 as the Four Aims, by lead singer Levi Stubbs, Abdul "Duke" Fakir, Renaldo "Obie" Benson, and Lawrence Payton?

    a. The Four Tops
    b. The Four Seasons
    c. The Temptations
    d. The Miracles

11. Name the two artists who recorded the classic 1982 duet "Up Where We Belong"?

12. Who am I?

I am an American singer and songwriter born in Phoenix, Arizona, in 1948.

Despite my successful solo career - which began with the release of my debut solo album *Bella Donna* in 1981 - I am perhaps best known for my work with the rock band I joined in 1975, who have gone on to sell more than 120 million records worldwide.

I wrote a number of the band's biggest and most popular hits, including "Landslide" and "Dreams."

13. In the Nat King Cole hit "L-O-V-E," "O is for…" what?

    a. The open door
    b. The only one
    c. The ordinary
    d. The out and in

14. Which legendary music artist is the only person in history to have won an Oscar, a Grammy, the Presidential Medal of Freedom, and the Nobel Prize for Literature?

15. Whose albums include *Empty Sky, Caribou, Sleeping with the Past,* and *Made in England*?

    a. Elton John
    b. Phil Collins
    c. Sting
    d. U2

SOLUTIONS

1. A. "Don't Be Cruel." The single went on to sell more than six million copies. "Heartbreak Hotel" was the A-side to "I Was the One" in 1956; "All Shook Up" was released as the A-side to "That's When Your Heartaches Begin" in 1957; and "Treat Me Nice" was the B-side to 1957's "Jailhouse Rock."
2. False. Actually, the Boss has never had a Number 1. His biggest chart success, "Dancing in the Dark," only reached Number 2 in 1984.
3. B. Jimmy Ruffin.
4. B. "Walk Like a Man" (The Four Seasons, 1963), D. "The Way We Were" (Barbra Streisand, 1974), C. "Say You, Say Me" (Lionel Richie, 1985), A. "Save the Best for Last" (Vanessa Williams, 1992).

5. D. 96. Question Mark? and the Mysterians' hit was the second biggest-selling track of the year, behind The Mamas and the Papas' "California Dreamin'."
6. B. 1956.
7. D. Celine Dion
8. C. Matt Monro.
9. B. Hank Williams Jr.
10. A. The Four Tops.
11. Joe Cocker and Jennifer Warnes.
12. Stevie Nicks.
13. B. The only one. "L is for the way you look at me / O is for the only one I see, / V is very, very extraordinary / E is even more than anyone that you adore can."
14. Bob Dylan. Dylan was awarded the Medal of Freedom by President Obama in 2012 and was also awarded the 2016 Nobel Prize. He

won an Oscar for the track "Things Have Changed" in 2001.

15. A. Elton John.

DID YOU KNOW?

- As well as his pet chimpanzee Bubbles, Michael Jackson kept two llamas named Lola and Louis. He once took the pair into his recording studio to meet Freddie Mercury!
- When working on their cover version of the famous power ballad "All By Myself," music producer David Foster arranged the song far higher than Celine Dion had been expecting to sing it, requiring her to now hit the note F5 (two Fs above middle C).
- Despite stiff competition from the likes of Madonna and Taylor Swift, the first solo artist to gross more than $100 million was actually Tina Turner, with her Twenty-Four Seven World Tour in 1995.
- Only three artists in pop history have sold over 100 million albums globally both as part of a band, and as a solo artist: Phil

Collins, Paul McCartney, and Michael Jackson.

- The Bee Gees were originally called The Rattlesnakes, Nirvana was once called Skid Row, Def Leppard were founded as a band called Atomic Mass - and Simon and Garfunkel originally recorded under the name Tom and Jerry!

What is Sisyphus' favorite band?

– The Rolling Stones!

ROUND 4

MAKING HISTORY

A lot has changed in the last eight decades or so - and this round is here to test your knowledge and your memory of it!

See how you get on with these 15 questions all about the major events, people, and places of the past 80 years of world history.

1. Work this out: What are the next two letters on this list?

   RN
   GF
   JC
   RR
   ?

2. In what decade were the floppy disk, laser, and high-speed rail all introduced?

   a. 1950s
   b. 1960s
   c. 1970s

d. 1980s

3. Name three of the five codenames used for the beaches of the D-Day Normandy Landings in 1944.

4. Which country began its Great Leap Forward in 1958?

   a. Russia
   b. Italy
   c. China
   d. Mexico

5. One of the first anti-Communist revolutions of the Cold War era was instigated by students in what European country in 1956?

   a. Greece
   b. Poland
   c. Hungary
   d. Czechoslovakia

6. Who was Queen Elizabeth II's father, who was her predecessor on the British throne?

a. Edward VI
b. Edward VIII
c. George V
d. George VI

7. True or False?

   John F Kennedy is the youngest person in history to hold the office of US president.

8. The famous Brown v. Board ruling of the Supreme Court in 1954 declared that laws establishing racially segregated schools unconstitutional - in what US city?

   a. Oklahoma City
   b. Topeka
   c. Madison
   d. Des Moines

9. Introduced in 1948, the Marshall Plan was designed to rebuild the countries and economies of the Axis nations after World War II. But who was "Marshall"?

   a. UK Foreign Office leader

b. US Secretary of State
c. Canadian Prime Minister
d. French President

10. Who am I?

Born in a tiny Russian village in 1894, I trained as a metal worker before becoming involved in politics under Joseph Stalin.

After serving in Ukraine in the 1930s, I was called back to Moscow and served as one of Stalin's closest advisors until his death in 1953.

At that point, I was made the first secretary of the Communist Party of the Soviet Union and became the 7th Premier of the Soviet Union in 1958 - whereupon I became known for my surprising denunciation of Stalin's politics and embarked on a modernizing "de-Stalinization" of the Soviet world.

I remained in power until 1964 and died seven years later in 1971.

11. The Berlin Wall came down in 1989 - but when was it built?

    a. 1941
    b. 1951
    c. 1961
    d. 1971

12. Put these four events of the 1970s in order from earliest to latest.

    a. The death of Elvis
    b. The Watergate Scandal
    c. Election of Margaret Thatcher, the UK's first female prime minister
    d. Roe v. Wade

13. Following the election of Mrs. Thatcher, the UK has now had two more female Prime Ministers. Name both for a point each.

14. What 20th-century conflict was conducted in two phases, named Operation Desert Shield and Operation Desert Storm?

    a. Korean War
    b. Vietnam War
    c. Falklands War
    d. Gulf War

15. In what year did John Hinckley, Jr. attempt to assassinate Ronald Reagan?

    a. 1980
    b. 1981
    c. 1982
    d. 1983

SOLUTIONS

1. GB. In chronological order, these are the initials of the successive US presidents Richard Nixon, Gerald Ford, Jimmy Carter, and Ronald Reagan. Next on the list would be George Bush.
2. B. 1960s. IBM developed the first eight-inch floppy disks in the early 60s; the first laser was invented in 1960; and the world's first high-speed rail commercial passenger service, Japan's Shinkansen train, went into operation in 1964.
3. Pick three from Utah, Omaha, Gold, Juno, and Sword.
4. C. China.
5. C. Hungary. More than 5,000 students invaded a civic hall in Budapest, demanding the withdrawal of Soviet troops from the

country and the re-establishment of free elections on October 22, 1956.

6. D. George VI.
7. False. At 43 years old, Kennedy remains the youngest person ever *elected* US president - but Theodore Roosevelt was just 42 when he unexpectedly assumed office on the death of William McKinley in 1901.
8. B. Topeka.
9. B. US Secretary of State. The plan was overseen by President Truman's Secretary of State, George C Marshall. For his work on the plan, Marshall was awarded the Nobel Peace Prize in 1953.
10. Nikita Khrushchev
11. C. 1961.
12. B. The Watergate scandal (1972), D. Roe v. Wade (1973), A. The death of Elvis (1977), C. Election of Margaret Thatcher, the UK's first female prime minister (1979).

13. Theresa May (2016-19) and Liz Truss (2022).
14. D. Gulf War. Desert Shield was the initial military build-up carried out from August 1990 to January 1991, followed by Desert Storm - the aerial bombardment of Saddam Hussein's Iraq.
15. A. 1980.

DID YOU KNOW?

- The first patient ever treated with the newly discovered antibiotic penicillin was a 43-year-old British police officer named Albert Alexander, who had an infected rosebush scratch on his face.
- During World War II, a bear served in the Polish army!
- In 1967, the first person ever to receive a heart transplant lived just 18 days after the procedure. However, the medical techniques and technologies involved in the procedure improved so rapidly over the year that followed that the second patient, the following year, survived 18 *months*!
- Queen Elizabeth II spoke fluent French and was a trained mechanic.
- At the funeral of Ronald Reagan in 2004, Margaret Thatcher gave a eulogy and was seated beside Mikhail Gorbachev.

Why did Germany lose World War II?

– Well, it's three Reichs, and you're out!

ROUND 5

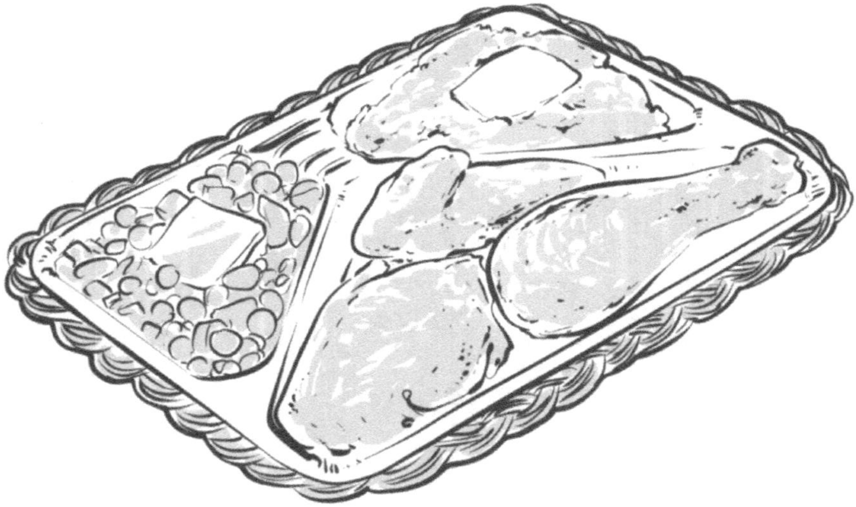

GADGETS & TECH

Time seems to go by faster as you get older, and one thing that makes that seem ever more real is the ever-changing world of technology!

There were no iPhones, iPads, digital televisions, or world wide web back in the 1950s, after all!

No matter how much of a techy you are, though, see how you get on with this round of questions all about the gadgets and gizmos of the last eight years - some of which you might have long forgotten about!

1. Which of these first went on sale in 1946?
    a. Tupperware
    b. Microwave
    c. Cuisinart
    d. Non-stick pan
2. William L Maxson's frozen dinners were invented in 1944 and are considered the

world's first microwave meals. Where were they served?

a. Hospitals
b. Airplanes
c. Schools
d. Prisons

3. True or False? The character you operate on in the game *Operation* is called Milburn Pennybags.

4. What did the H in the video system VHS stand for?

a. High
b. Holding
c. Hydrogen
d. Home

5. Put the following four 20th-century gadgets in the order of their introduction to the market, from earliest to latest.

a. Camcorder
b. Polaroid camera

c. Color photocopier
d. Lava lamp

6. What am I?

I was invented by accident in 1958, when a Kansas Dairy Queen franchise owner named Omar Knedlik forgot about several bottles of soda he had placed in the freezer to cool down, causing them to freeze overnight. When the icy drinks inadvertently proved a hit with his customers, Oman began to sell them under the name "Icee," and patented a machine to make them.

When the rights to the machine were sold to 7-Eleven in 1965, my name was changed to the name I'm still sold under today!

7. Introduced in 1954, the Constellation was a classic type of what household device?

a. Vacuum cleaner
b. Electric heater

c. Desk lamp
d. Washing machine

8. True or False?

   Bubblewrap was invented in the 1950s by two engineers trying to develop three-dimensional wallpaper.

9. In 1974, what became the first product in the world sold with a barcode?

   a. Toothpaste
   b. Lipstick
   c. Canned soup
   d. Chewing gum

10. The world's first *what* was installed at a branch of Barclays Bank in London on 27 June 1967?

    a. Coin sorting machine
    b. Walk-through metal-detecting security gates
    c. Silent security alarm
    d. ATM

11. In what year was the compact disk introduced?

    a. 1962
    b. 1972
    c. 1982
    d. 1992

12. Introduced in 1972, what was the Magnavox Odyssey?

    a. Word processor
    b. Video games console
    c. Electric oven
    d. Television set

13. What was the name of the supersonic airliner that entered scheduled operations across the Atlantic in 1976?

14. Dot matrix was an early form of what item of office equipment?

    a. Printer
    b. Shredder
    c. File cabinet

d. Fax machine

15. Which company introduced the Walkman portable cassette tape player in 1979?

    a. Sony
    b. Bose
    c. Ericsson
    d. Panasonic

SOLUTIONS

1. A. Tupperware.
2. B. Airplanes.
3. False. Milburn Pennybags is the character on the *Monopoly* box. The character in *Operation* is called Cavity Sam.
4. D. Home. VHS stands for Video Home System.
5. B. Polaroid camera (1948), D. Lava lamp (1963), C. Color photocopier (1973), A. Camcorder (1983).
6. Slurpee.
7. A. Vacuum cleaner. The Hoover company's round Constellation cleaner was discontinued after 20 years in 1975.
8. True!
9. D. Chewing gum. The UPC, or Universal Product Code, first appeared on a package

of Wrigley's gum that went on sale in Marsh's Supermarket in Troy, Ohio, in June 1974.

10. D. ATM. As part of the publicity drive around the ATM opening, the first person to withdraw cash from an ATM was the British actor and comedian Reg Varney.
11. C. 1982.
12. B. Video game console. The Odyssey was the home entertainment system that brought the first video game, *Pong*, into American homes.
13. Concorde. Having cut transatlantic flights from seven or eight hours to three-and-a-half hours from New York to Paris, the aircraft was retired amid growing security concerns in 2003.
14. A. Printer.
15. A. Sony.

DID YOU KNOW?

- The whirling globules inside a lava lamp are mainly made from paraffin wax.
- Although the food mixer is now synonymous with the 1970s brand Cuisinart, the very first electric mixer was introduced more than two decades earlier by Starmix in 1946!
- Post-It Notes were invented by accident in when a chemist named Spencer Silver tried to make a super-strong adhesive, and instead inadvertently produced a super-weak adhesive, which could be used to only stick things together temporarily and be easily removed without leaving any residue. Initially seeing no purpose for his creation, the adhesive sat unused in the 3M laboratories until the idea for the Post-It was conceived of in 1973.

- The first liquid paper was invented by Bette Nesmith Graham - the mother of 'Monkees' guitarist Michael Nesmith - in her kitchen in 1956.
- The microwave oven was invented in 1945, when an engineer named Percy Spencer began tinkering with a radar machine and noticed that a chocolate bar in his shirt pocket had melted!

Why is bubble wrap so popular with kids?
– It's a big part of pop culture!

ROUND 6

THE 60S AND 70S

We have had a look at the 40s and 50s, and now we're skipping forward in time to the heady decades of the 1960s and 70s.

See how you get on with this round of questions dedicated to the postwar era.

1. The most powerful nuclear weapon ever tested was detonated in the skies above what country in 1961?
    a. China
    b. Australia
    c. Russia
    d. United States
2. Who was US president in 1960, and who was US president in 1970?

    Get one point for each name.
3. Who married Greek shipping magnate Aristotle Onassis in 1968?

a. Audrey Hepburn
b. Jackie Kennedy
c. Barbra Streisand
d. Margaret Chase Smith

4. In 1963, Justice Lorna Lockwood became the first woman in US history to serve as chief justice of a state supreme court. But what state was it?

    a. California
    b. Arizona
    c. Florida
    d. Kentucky

5. True or False?

    In 1967, Muhammad Ali was unceremoniously stripped of his World Boxing Title.

6. In what city is Candlestick Park, the site of the Beatles' final proper concert on August 29, 1966?

    a. New York

b. Chicago
c. San Francisco
d. Phoenix

7. Who defeated the Kansas City Chiefs 35-10 to win Super Bowl I in 1967?

   a. Green Bay Packers
   b. San Diego Chargers
   c. San Francisco 49ers
   d. Baltimore Colts

8. What California city elected Doris A Davis, the United States' first Black woman mayor, in 1973?

   a. Compton
   b. Fresno
   c. Bakersfield
   d. Modesto

9. What was the average price of a gallon of milk in 1970?

   a. 69 ¢
   b. $1.32

c. $1.90

d. $2.22

10. Who was “Tired of Being Alone” in 1971?

a. Rod Stewart

b. Bee Gees

c. James Taylor

d. Al Green

11. Of what African country was Idi Amin leader from 1971-1979?

a. Tanzania

b. Algeria

c. Zimbabwe

d. Uganda

12. American nationals living on what European island were evacuated in 1974 following a Greek coup d’état and a subsequent Turkish invasion?

a. Sicily

b. Malta

c. Cyprus

d. Crete

13. The Six-Day War of 1967 was a short-lived conflict between a coalition of Arab nations - including Egypt and Syria - and what other Middle East country?

    a. Bahrain
    b. Israel
    c. Saudi Arabia
    d. Jordan

14. Which of these major companies was founded in Albuquerque in 1976?

    a. Microsoft
    b. CNN
    c. HarperCollins
    d. Dell

15. In what Latin American country did the infamous Jamestown Massacre of 1979 take place?

    a. Brazil
    b. Ecuador

c. Chile

d. Guyana

SOLUTIONS

1. C. Russia. The 60,000 lb bomb AN602 - known as the "Tsar Bomba" - was developed by Soviet physicist Andrei Sakharov. It had an equivalent power almost four times that of the "Little Boy" bomb dropped on Hiroshima in 1945.
2. Dwight D Eisenhower and Richard Nixon.
3. B. Jackie Kennedy.
4. B. Arizona.
5. True. On April 28, 1967, Ali refused to be drafted into the US Army and had his heavyweight title immediately removed as a result.
6. C. San Francisco
7. A. Green Bay Packers
8. A. Compton.
9. B. $1.32.

10. D. Al Green.

11. D. Uganda.

12. C. Cyprus. The island has been divided between the Greek-supported and internationally recognized independent Republic of Cyprus and the Turkish Republic of Northern Cyprus ever since.

13. B. Israel.

14. A. Microsoft.

15. D. Guyana.

DID YOU KNOW?

- The Beatles' actual last concert was not a regular gig but an impromptu outdoor performance on the rooftop of their Apple Records headquarters on Savile Row in London.
- The global population in 1960 was just three billion. In 2023, it surpassed eight billion.
- Gasoline was only 36 cents per gallon in 1970!
- The so-called Outer Space Treaty was introduced worldwide at the height of the space race in 1967. As this was also at the height of the Cold War, the Treaty forbids the weaponization of space and the Moon - while Article VIII states that a person can be arrested for a crime committed anywhere in the known universe!
- When it was released in 1977, George Lucas was so sure that *Star Wars* would be a flop

that instead of going to the premiere, he and his friend Steven Spielberg went on holiday to Hawaii!

What did the other Beatles say when John Lennon got married?

– Oh no!

ROUND 7

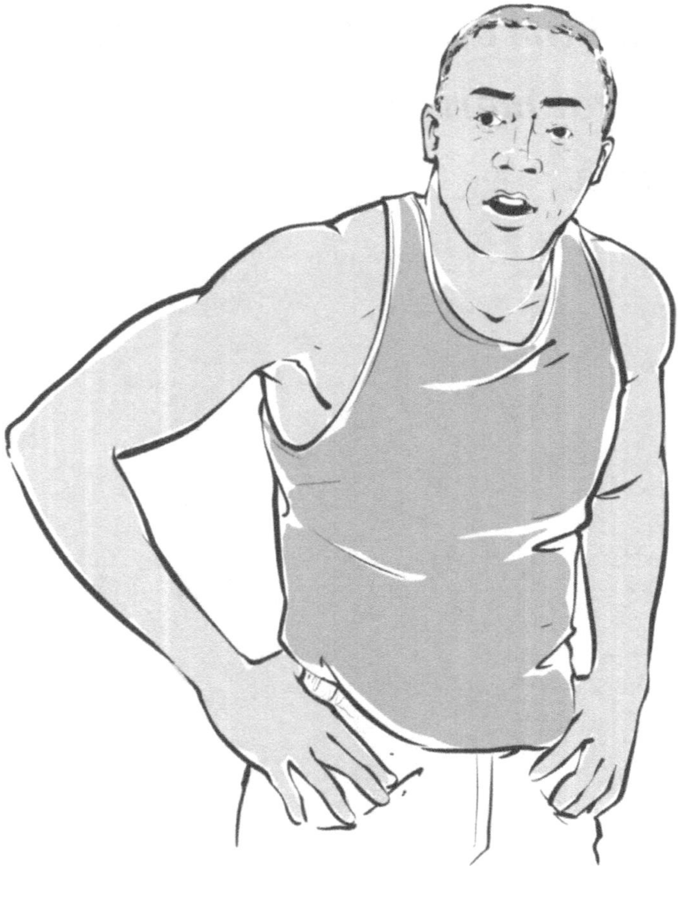

SPORTS & GAMES

The past 80 years have seen some remarkable sportsmen and women take to the world stage - and some truly remarkable sporting events take place all over the globe.

From boxing and basketball to the Summer Olympic Games, test your knowledge of the last eight decades of sporting prowess with this round of questions…

1. Which racehorse won the Santa Anita Handicap on his final race in March 1940?
    a. Twilight Fear
    b. Seabiscuit
    c. Cavalcade
    d. Sword Dancer
2. In what discipline did Romanian Nadia Comăneci become a five-time Olympic gold medalist?
    a. Gymnastics

b. Marathon
c. Archery
d. Javelin

3. Put these famous sporting figures in order of their birth, from earliest to latest.

    a. Tiger Woods
    b. Kurt Browning
    c. Carl Lewis
    d. Mark Spitz

4. When they defeated the San Diego Chargers 49-26 at Super Bowl XXIX in 1995, who became the first team in history to win five Super Bowl championships?

    a. Los Angeles Raiders
    b. Chicago Bears
    c. Pittsburgh Steelers
    d. San Francisco 49ers

5. There were two Summer Olympic Games held in the 1970s - one in 1972, and another four years later in 1976 - both of which were

hosted by cities with names beginning with M. Name both the host cities for a point each!

6. Who hit his 500th home run on May 14, 1967, to become the sixth member of the 500-home run club?

    a. Joe Pepitone
    b. Hank Aaron
    c. Mickey Mantle
    d. Willie Mays

7. In 1971, who became the first golfer in history to win the PGA Championship twice?

    a. Nick Faldo
    b. Gary Player
    c. Dave Stockton
    d. Jack Nicklaus

8. Who am I?

I am an American professional baseball right fielder, born in Mobile, Alabama, in 1934.

I played in 23 seasons of Major League Baseball beginning in 1954 and running through to 1976. Of those seasons, 21 were with the Atlanta Braves; the other two were with the Milwaukee Brewers.

One of the many highlights of my career was breaking Babe Ruth's long-standing MLB record for career home runs - a record I held for the next 33 years, until 2007.

I died in 2021, at the age of 86.

9. What country was banned from the Olympic Games for 32 years, before making their return to international sport at the Barcelona Games in 1992?

    a. Russia
    b. South Africa
    c. China

d. Zimbabwe

10. Which tennis ace has won a record 14 French Open titles?

    a. Pete Sampras
    b. Rafael Nadal
    c. Novak Djokovic
    d. Roger Federer

11. In 1968, athlete Jim Hines became the first person in history to run what distance and in what time?

    a. 100m in less than ten seconds
    b. 400m in less than 45 seconds
    c. One mile in less than four minutes
    d. A marathon in less than two-and-a-half hours

12. Sir Steve Redgrave is a legendary name in what water sport?

    a. Diving
    b. Water polo
    c. Rowing

d. Yachting

13. True or False?

    In 1984, German athlete Uwe Hohn became the first and only competitive athlete to throw a javelin more than 100m.

14. Which boxer was unexpectedly knocked out in the tenth round of a bout with relative unknown James "Buster" Douglas in Tokyo in 1990?

    a. George Foreman
    b. Frank Bruno
    c. Mike Tyson
    d. Michael Moorer

15. In what state is the 106,000-capacity Beaver Stadium, the second-largest stadium in the United States?

    a. California
    b. Pennsylvania
    c. Florida
    d. Tennessee

SOLUTIONS

1. B. Seabiscuit. The prize was $121,000!
2. A. Gymnastics. In 1976 - at the age of just 14 - Comăneci became the first gymnast in history to be awarded a perfect score of 10.0.
3. D. Mark Spitz (1950), C. Carl Lewis (1961), B. Kurt Browning (1966), A. Tiger Woods (1975).
4. D. San Francisco 49ers.
5. Munich and Montreal.
6. C. Mickey Mantle. Babe Ruth became the first 500 Club member in 1929, followed by Jimmie Foxx (1940), Mel Ott (1945), Ted Williams (1960), and Willie Mays (1965). Mantle was joined just a matter of weeks later by Eddie Matthews, who hit his 500th home run on July 14, 1967.
7. D. Jack Nicklaus.

8. Hank Aaron.
9. B. South Africa. The International Olympic Committee only reinvited South Africa to take part in the Olympic Games after the end of the apartheid system in the early 1990s.
10. B. Rafael Nadal. Roger Federer has won a record eight Wimbledon titles, while Djokovic is the Australian Open record holder with ten titles.
11. A. 100m in less than ten seconds. Hines' time was 9.95 seconds. His record stood for almost 15 years.
12. C. Rowing. Redgrave won gold medals in rowing at five consecutive Olympic Games, from 1984 to 2000.
13. True. Hohn's throw - 343 feet, 9¾ inches - remains a record, and likely always will: the design of competitive javelins was changed two years after his throw, making the

official javelin heavier and with a different center of gravity. Therefore, any future 100m+ throws are highly unlikely.

14. C. Mike Tyson.
15. B. Pennsylvania. Beaver Stadium has been home to the Penn State Nittany Lions since 1960. It is second in capacity only to Michigan Stadium in Ann Arbor and is not only the second-largest stadium in the US, but the entire Western Hemisphere!

DID YOU KNOW?

- In 1943, the Pittsburgh Steelers and the Philadelphia Eagles both had so many players drafted into World War II that the remaining teammates decided to join forces and played as "The Steagles" for the rest of the season.
- The shortest person ever to play in the NBA, Muggsy Bogues, is five feet three inches tall!
- In 1963, Hall of Fame pitcher Gaylord Perry famously stated that, "They'll put a man on the Moon before I hit a home run!" Six years later, Perry hit his first and only home run just hours after Neil Armstrong stepped out onto the surface of the Moon!
- Olympic gold medals have not been solid gold since 1912. They are now mainly silver coated in gold plate.
- Theodore Roosevelt was so concerned with sports injuries that he reportedly threatened

to ban football unless the NFL improved player safety.

Why did the golfer wear two pairs of pants?

– He got a hole in one!

ROUND 8

SCHOOL DAYS

This section of our quiz is something of a mixed bag… or rather, a mixed school bag!

The focus in this round is on all the kinds of things you might have learned about in school (and hopefully haven't forgotten since then!) From math tests to history class, and from science to citizenship, let's see if you can remember these basic schooltime facts and figures…

1. If a, b, and c are the three sides of a right triangle, whose theorem states that $a^2 + b^2 = c^2$ (or, put another way, $c = \sqrt{a^2 + b^2}$)?

    a. Newton
    b. Archimedes
    c. Pythagoras
    d. Euclid

2. King Henry VIII and King James I of England belonged to two different consecutive royal houses.

   Name them for a point each.

3. Which of these is NOT an irregular verb?

   a. Buy
   b. Catch
   c. Place
   d. Give

4. Ratified in 1933, the 21st Amendment to the US Constitution repealed an earlier amendment. Which one?

   a. 5th
   b. 11th
   c. 18th
   d. 20th

5. Which Shakespeare play features four lovers named Lysander, Demetrius, Helena, and Hermia?

a. *A Midsummer Night's Dream*
b. *Twelfth Night*
c. *Love's Labour's Lost*
d. *Much Ado About Nothing*

6. What will you always find at the end of an interrogative sentence?

    a. A period
    b. A question mark
    c. An exclamation point
    d. A person's name

7. What does the A in DNA stand for?

    a. Amylase
    b. Alkali
    c. Antigen
    d. Acid

8. In math, $4/3 \pi r^3$ - where r is the radius - is the formula for working out… what?

    a. Height of a cone
    b. Diameter of a circle
    c. Base of a cylinder

d. Area of a sphere

9. Who am I?

I was born in the Italian city of Pisa, which at the time was part of the independent Duchy of Florence, in 1564. Although I had planned to enter the priesthood, I was encouraged by my father to study medicine at university and instead began a long and illustrious career in science.

Among the areas of study, I participated in were gravitational forces, speed, velocity, and inertia, and I am also credited with inventing several new devices, including improved lenses and microscopes, and a type of military compass.

It is for my work in astronomy that I am best remembered, however, as it was I who either discovered or first observed the four largest moons of Jupiter, the rings of Saturn, the phases of the planet Venus, sunspots, and lunar craters.

My work brought me into conflict with the Catholic Church at the time, as I believed the Earth revolved around the Sun, not the other way around. For that, I fell afoul of the Inquisition in the mid-1600s. As a result, I spent the final decades of my life under house arrest before my death in 1642.

10. There are four elements on the periodic table whose names begin with I. Name two of the four for a point each.

11. In music, how is the treble clef symbol also known?

    a. C clef
    b. E clef
    c. F clef
    d. G clef

12. Which revolutionary figurehead and Founding Father of the United States wrote the 1776 pamphlet "Common Sense"?

    a. Benjamin Franklin

b. John Adams
c. Thomas Paine
d. Robert Morris

13. Peristalsis is a rhythmic movement involved in what bodily process?

    a. Digestion
    b. Circulation
    c. Respiration
    d. Rest

14. Who wrote *Vanity Fair*?

    a. Jane Austen
    b. William Makepeace Thackeray
    c. Charles Dickens
    d. George Eliot

15. True or False?

    The first state to ratify the US Constitution was Pennsylvania.

SOLUTIONS

1. C. Pythagoras. In any right triangle, the square of the longest side or hypotenuse, opposite the right angle (c), is equal to the sum of the squares of the other two sides (a, b).
2. Tudor and Stuart.
3. C. Place.
4. C. 18th. The 18th Amendment prohibited the production and sale of alcohol. It was repealed at the end of the Prohibition Era, a little over 14 years later.
5. A. *A Midsummer Night's Dream*.
6. B. A question mark. Interrogatives pose questions; declarative sentences are straightforward statements.
7. D. Acid. DNA is deoxyribonucleic acid.
8. D. Area of a sphere.

9. Galileo.
10. Take two from indium, iodine, iridium, or iron.
11. D. G clef.
12. C. Thomas Paine.
13. A. Digestion. Although the term can be used for other organs and ducts of the body, peristalsis is particularly associated with the alternating contraction and relaxation of the intestines, which pushes digested food further through the digestive system.
14. B. William Makepeace Thackeray.
15. False. It was Delaware, on December 7, 1787. Pennsylvania was second, on December 12.

DID YOU KNOW?

- The average relationship of high-school teens lasts less than five months.
- Only four high schools in the entire United States have a graduation rate of 100%.
- Six in ten high school graduates go on to college and further education.
- California has more high schools than any other US state, and its 6,000,000 school students are taught by a quarter of a million teachers.
- Dropping out of high school is not the end of the world… Among the many famous high school dropouts are Microsoft founder and philanthropist Bill Gates, media tycoon Oprah Winfrey, Oscar-winning actor Jennifer Lawrence, and Walt Disney. Most illustrious of all, however, is Albert Einstein: the future Nobel Prize-winner dropped out of high school at age 15, before

reconsidering his decision and sitting the entrance exam to the prestigious Swiss Institute of Technology the following year. He failed the exam. (Though he did pass it on his second attempt the following year!)

Why did the school kid eat his math test?
– Because the teacher told him it was a piece of cake...

ROUND 9

FAMOUS PEOPLE

We have already encountered some well-known names and faces on the way here, but this round is dedicated entirely to the historical figures whose impact on the last 80 years has been bigger than most.

1. In what city did Martin Luther King deliver his famous "I Have a Dream" speech?

    a. Boston
    b. Washington, D.C.
    c. Philadelphia
    d. New York

2. True or False?

    Mary Tyler Moore's first television appearance was playing an elf in a Hotpoint commercial.

3. Put these four television hosts in order of the year they were born, beginning with the oldest.

a. Stephen Colbert
b. David Letterman
c. Larry King
d. Jay Leno

4. Which British musician and music producer was Annie Lennox's partner in the pop group Eurhythmics?

   a. Dave Stewart
   b. Phil Collins
   c. Peter Gabriel
   d. Mike Batt

5. Two of the four stars of *The Golden Girls* had earlier appeared together in the 1970s CBS sitcom *Maude*. Name both for a point each.

6. What was US baseball star Cal Ripken's nickname?

   a. Iron Man
   b. Batman
   c. Spider-Man
   d. Aquaman

7. Who am I?

I am an American statesman and eventual president who was born in Texas in 1908. I assumed the presidency under extraordinary circumstances, having earlier served the state of Texas in the House of Representatives in the 1930s and 40s, and worked as Senator for Texas from 1949 to 1961 - during which time I was Senate Majority Whip from 1951 to 1953.

I was the United States' 37th Vice President and its 36th President; unusually, for the first two years of my presidency, I worked without a vice president myself, before Hubert Humphrey took the office for the final four years of my term.

Having left the presidency after my second successful term, tragically I died suddenly of heart failure in 1973, at the age of 64.

8. In 2001, which Irish artist's hit single "Only Time" - from the album *A Day Without Rain* - took on significant meaning after its use alongside news footage of the September 11 attacks in New York City?

   a. U2
   b. The Corrs
   c. Enya
   d. Clannad

9. Which actress won her second Oscar for the movie *Blue Jasmine* in 2013?

   a. Jennifer Lawrence
   b. Cate Blanchett
   c. Julia Roberts
   d. Annette Benning

10. Indira Gandhi became the first female prime minister of what country in 1966?

   a. Israel
   b. Thailand
   c. Pakistan

d. India

11. In what year did Muhammad Ali officially change his name from Cassius Clay, having announced his conversion to Islam?

    a. 1958
    b. 1964
    c. 1969
    d. 1975

12. True or False?

    When NASA first opened applications for its Apollo 11 program, aiming to take the first astronauts to the Moon in the late 1960s, Neil Armstrong's was the very first application to be submitted.

13. Who was the President of France from 1959 to 1969?

    a. George Pompidou
    b. Jacques Chirac
    c. Charles de Gaulle
    d. René Coty

14. Which famous Oscar-winning movie director began his career as an actor and played Richie Cunningham in *Happy Days*?

    a. Steven Spielberg
    b. Ron Howard
    c. George Lucas
    d. Brian De Palma

15. In what country did Bette Davis die in 1989?

    a. Mexico
    b. Australia
    c. France
    d. UK

SOLUTIONS

1. B. Washington, D.C.
2. True! In her teens, Moore starred as an elf named "Happy Hotpoint" in a series of over 30 household appliance commercials.
3. C. Larry King (1933), B. David Letterman (1947), D. Jay Leno (1950), A. Stephen Colbert (1964).
4. A. Dave Stewart.
5. Bea Arthur and Rue McClanahan. Bea Arthur (who would go on to play Dorothy in *The Golden Girls*) played the title role in *Maude*, while McClanahan (who played Blanche) starred alongside her as Maude's next-door neighbor Vivian.
6. A. Iron Man.
7. Lyndon B Johnson.

8. C. Enya. After sales of the single increased in the aftermath of the attacks, Enya donated her earnings from the song to the Widows' and Children's Fund of the Uniformed Firefighters Association, which assisted the families of firefighters killed in the aftermath of the attacks.
9. B. Cate Blanchett.
10. D. India. Mrs. Gandhi served three consecutive terms as Indian prime minister from 1966 to 1977, and then a fourth from 1980 to 1984.
11. B. 1964.
12. False. In fact, Armstrong sent his application in late, and it arrived a week after the deadline. He was only considered for inclusion after one of his friends and former colleagues secretly moved his application into the pile of those that had arrived on time!

13. C. Charles de Gaulle.

14. B. Ron Howard.

15. C. France.

DID YOU KNOW?

- Bette Davis' 1950 role in *All About Eve* - for which she received her record ninth Oscar nomination - almost wasn't hers. The role had originally gone to Claudette Colbert, but after she injured her back filming *Three Came Home* (1950), she was forced to drop out of the role, which was handed to Davis at the last minute.
- In the original pitch for *The Mary Tyler Moore Show,* Moore's character was intended to be a recently divorced woman starting out on her own again in later life. As divorce was still a controversial issue in the 1960s - and the producers were worried that viewers might think Moore's character must have split from her on-screen husband in the earlier *Dick Van Dyke Show* - the character was rewritten!

- Lyndon Johnson was sworn in as president on board Air Force One, just hours after the death of John F Kennedy. Jackie Kennedy was one of the witnesses to Johnson's inauguration, as was his wife, Lady Bird.
- Before changing his name to Muhammad Ali, Cassius Clay was briefly known as Cassius X - a placeholder name used after Ali abandoned his surname, claiming that it was a "slave name" to which he no longer wished to be attached.
- Before she became a famous actress, Bea Arthur served as a truck driver in the United States Marine Corps Women's Reserve in World War II.

How did Muhammad Ali feel after drinking a bottle of soda too quickly?
– Gaseous Clay!

ROUND 10

FOOD AND DRINK

Here is another something of a mixed bag round - albeit this time, a grocery bag!

Food and drink trends have changed a lot over the last 80 years, and from Chef Boyardee to TV dinners, this round of questions is designed to test your knowledge of all of it.

Bon Appetit!

1. What shape is farfalle pasta?
    a. Spirals
    b. Quills
    c. Bowtie
    d. Shells
2. What was the average price of a carton of a dozen eggs in 1970?
    a. 60 ¢
    b. 90 ¢
    c. $1.10

d. $1.55

3. Who am I?

I am an American chef and cookery writer, who was born in Pasadena, California, in 1912. My maiden name was McWilliams.

A keen sportswoman in college, I had originally planned to become novelist and took a job as a copywriter in New York after graduation. During the war, I was found to be too tall to serve in the Women's Army Corps, and so I worked as a typist for the Office of Strategic Services in Washington instead.

Through my work at the OSS, I met my husband, Paul, and after the war, we relocated to France where I began collecting recipes and writing about French cookery.

I published my guide to French cuisine in 1961; it was while publicizing the book on television that I caught the attention of a producers and was later hired to front my own cookery program in 1963.

After a lengthy career both behind and in front of the camera, I retired in 2001 and died three years later - just two days short of my 92nd birthday!

4. What soft drink was originally marketed as a temperance drink and medicinal preparation in the late 1800s?
    a. Pepsi
    b. Coca-Cola
    c. Fanta
    d. Mountain Dew
5. Which of these is NOT a traditional component of Eggs Benedict?
    a. Hollandaise sauce
    b. English muffin
    c. Bacon
    d. Spinach

6. What is the traditional flavor of an aioli sauce?

    a. Garlic
    b. Honey
    c. Chili
    d. Seafood

7. True or False?

    There is more caffeine in a typical cup of tea than in a cup of coffee.

8. Put these four famous food brands in order of their first appearance on the market, oldest to most recent.

    a. Tropicana
    b. Diet Coke
    c. Cap'n Crunch
    d. Chef Boyardee

9. In what country are Chupa Chups' candies manufactured?

    a. Mexico

b. Brazil
c. Argentina
d. Spain

10. Three of these cheeses are French, while the other is Swiss. Which is the odd one out?

    a. Camembert
    b. Emmenthal
    c. Reblochon
    d. Roquefort

11. Used as a creamy white base sauce for dishes like macaroni cheese, a traditional roux comprises just three ingredients (excluding seasoning).

    Name two of them for a point each.

12. The spice mace is made from the outer casing that surrounds the seeds of what other spice?

    a. Nutmeg
    b. Cumin
    c. Mustard

d. Anise

13. One cup of flour is generally taken to be equivalent to what more precise measure?

    a. 2 ounces
    b. 4½ ounces
    c. 6 ounces
    d. 9 ounces

14. In what decade was the Ben & Jerry's ice cream company founded?

    a. 1970s
    b. 1980s
    c. 1990s
    d. 2000s

15. True or False?

    Corn Flakes were invented by accident when a tray of boiled wheat mash was left to dry too long.

SOLUTIONS

1. C. Bowtie. It might be better known as bowtie pasta, but farfalle is actually the Italian word for "butterflies."
2. A. 60 ¢.
3. Julia Child.
4. B. Coca-Cola. Containing extracts from both the coca leaf and kola nut plants, Coca-Cola was chiefly marketed as a stimulant - not least because its original preparation, using coca plant extract, meant that a typical glass contained roughly nine milligrams of cocaine!
5. D. Spinach. The use of a green like spinach - often in place of the bacon - turns the dish into eggs Florentine.
6. A. Garlic. Aioli is a mayonnaise-like sauce made of garlic and olive oil.

7. False. This is an old urban myth, based on a common misunderstanding! Pound for pound there is more caffeine in unprepared tea than in coffee - but as less tea is needed to brew a cup than the amount of coffee required to make the same, a cup of coffee contains more caffeine.
8. D. Chef Boyardee (1928), A. Tropicana (1947), C. Cap'n Crunch (1963), B. Diet Coke (1982).
9. D. Spain.
10. B. Emmenthal
11. Flour, butter, and milk.
12. A. Nutmeg. Technically, mace is made from the dried and ground aril - a kind of outer skin - that surrounds the nutmeg seed.
13. B. 4½ ounces. Although standards differ, a dry cup measure of flour or a similar ingredient is typically said to be equal to 4½ oz.

14. A. 1970s. Ben & Jerry's was founded in Burlington, Vermont, in 1978.

15. True! The mash became brittle and splintered into pieces when rolled. When these shards of wheat were baked, they became yellow "flakes" that soon proved a hit at breakfast time!

DID YOU KNOW?

- The iconic Chupa Chups logo was designed by the artist Salvador Dalí in 1969.
- Unlike many other brands, the picture on a can of Chef Boyardee pasta sauce is a real person. Ettore "Hector" Boiardi - who was born in Piacenza, Italy, 1897 - founded the Boyardee company in 1928 with his brothers after the family relocated to the United States.
- The rooster on the front of a box of cornflakes is named Cornelius.
- In the late 1870s, Constantin Fahlberg, a chemistry student at Johns Hopkins University in Baltimore, found that his fingers had a slightly sweet taste after working all day with a harmless chemical called ortho-sulfobenzoic acid imide. Thinking he could market the idea, Fahlberg began mass-producing the chemical and

released it to market under the name saccharin.

- Swap the bacon on an eggs benedict for haggis, and you will have an Eggs Balmoral - named after one of the British royal family's main Scottish residences!

What do you call someone who has two boxes of cereal open at once?
– A cereal adulterer!

ROUND 11

THE 1980S AND 90S

Time for our last round of era-defining questions, this one bringing things rather more up to date.

We are heading back in time just as far as the 1980s and 1990s with this tricky test of your history knowledge…

1. For a point each, name both countries that briefly fought the Falklands War in the early 1980s.
2. The Berlin Wall fell in 1989 - after how many years dividing East and West Germany?
    a. 18 years
    b. 28 years
    c. 38 years
    d. 48 years

3. In what modern-day country is the Chernobyl nuclear reactor, which went into meltdown in 1984?

   a. Estonia
   b. Belarus
   c. Albania
   d. Ukraine

4. In 1983, the US military invaded what Caribbean island?

   a. Cuba
   b. Grenada
   c. Dominica
   d. Barbados

5. Margaret Thatcher was elected the UK's first female prime minister in 1979 and remained in power for the entire 1980s before being ousted from Downing Street in 1990. She was not, however, the world's first female elected head of state, as these four

countries had all had female leaders before the UK.

Can you put them in order, from earliest to latest, based on the date their first female head of state came to power?

a. Argentina
b. Israel
c. Sri Lanka
d. India

6. Who wed on the 29 July 1981?

a. Prince Charles and Lady Diana Spencer
b. Paul and Linda McCartney
c. Madonna and Sean Penn
d. Bruce Willis and Demi Moore

7. Sandra Day O'Connor became the United States' first female Supreme Court Justice in what year?

a. 1981
b. 1985
c. 1991

d. 1995

8. The HST was launched in 1990 - but what is it?

    a. Television network
    b. Submarine
    c. Telescope
    d. Weather balloon

9. True or False? Nelson Mandela was not given his first name by his parents - instead, it was his schoolteacher's choice.

10. All these pop acts released their debut singles in either the 1980s or 1990s. Can you put them in order, starting with the group that hit the Billboard charts at the earliest?

    a. Spice Girls
    b. Backstreet Boys
    c. New Kids on the Block
    d. Boys II Men

11. Which US city was struck by devastating riots in 1992?

a. Atlanta
b. Los Angeles
c. Chicago
d. Austin

12. In what year of the 1990s were impeachment proceedings launched against President Clinton?

    a. 1992
    b. 1994
    c. 1996
    d. 1998

13. One of these James Bond movies was released in the 1980s, while the others arrived in cinemas in the 1990s. Which is the odd one out?

    a. *Tomorrow Never Dies*
    b. *Goldeneye*
    c. *The World Is Not Enough*
    d. *Licence to Kill*

14. Who am I?

I was born in Washington, DC, in 1948. Educated at Harvard, following my military service in the 1960s and 70s I entered into politics and served as a member of the House of Representatives from 1977 to 1985, and as United States Senator from Tennessee from 1985 to 1993 - the year I became the 45th Vice President.

After my work in politics, I became involved in environmental activism and won the 2007 Nobel Peace Prize for my work fighting against climate change. I celebrated my 75th birthday in 2023.

15. In the early 1990s, Yugoslavia broke apart to form five independent nations. Name two of them for a point each!

SOLUTIONS

1. The UK and Argentina.
2. B. 28 years. It was erected in 1961.
3. D. Ukraine.
4. B. Grenada. The invasion - which also involved a coalition of nearby Caribbean nations - was the result of unrest in the Grenadian People's Revolutionary Government, which had led to the death of the island nation's prime minister, Maurice Bishop.
5. C. Sri Lanka (Mrs. Sirimavo Bandaranaike, 1960), D. India (Indira Gandhi, 1966), B. Israel (Golda Meir, 1969), A. Argentina (Isabel Perón, 1974).
6. A. Prince Charles and Lady Diana Spencer. The wedding was broadcast around the world to a global audience of three-quarters of a billion people.

7. A. 1981. Nominated under President Reagan, she served until her death in 2006.
8. C. Telescope. The HST is the famous Hubble space telescope, which has been providing information about the universe for over 30 years!
9. True! Nelson Mandela was of Xhosa descent, and his birth name was Rolihlahla Mandela. On his first day in school, the teacher gave every pupil in his class a new anglicized name and chose Nelson instead of Rolihlahla. The name stuck, and Mr. Mandela used it for the rest of his life.
10. C. New Kids on the Block (1986), D. Boys II Men (1991), B. Backstreet Boys (1995), A. Spice Girls (1996).
11. B. Los Angeles.
12. D. 1998.
13. D. *Licence to Kill. Licence to Kill* was the second of Timothy Dalton's two Bond

movies (following 1987's *The Living Daylights*) released back in 1989. The other three movies here - *Goldeneye* (1995), *Tomorrow Never Dies* (1997), and *The World Is Not Enough* (1999) - starred Pierce Brosnan. He would go on to make one more appearance as Bond (in 2002's *Die Another Day*) before Daniel Craig took over the role for the remake of *Casino Royal* in 2006.

14. Al Gore.

15. From north to south, the five former Yugoslav republics were originally (1) Slovenia, (2) Croatia, (3) Bosnia-Herzegovina, (4) Serbia and Montenegro (which was for a time still known as Yugoslavia), and (5) Macedonia. The area has continued to break apart, however, with Serbia and Montenegro now peacefully established as independent nations, and Kosovo now beginning to be partially recognized as an independent state too.

DID YOU KNOW?

- Before she entered politics, Margaret Thatcher trained as a chemist and had a career helping to develop soft-serve ice cream.
- In 1991, New Kids on the Block were at the height of their fame - and topped *Forbes'* list of the world's highest-paid entertainers, above the likes of Madonna and Michael Jackson.
- Al Gore's environmental documentary *An Inconvenient Truth* won the Academy Award for Best Documentary Feature in 2007. Although Gore wrote the movie, he was not given a production credit; if he had, he would be only the third person in history to have won an Oscar and a Nobel Prize - alongside George Bernard Shaw and Bob Dylan!

- The Spice Girls' debut smash hit "Wannabe" was reportedly written in around ten minutes!
- The breakup of the Balkan states of Yugoslavia has been so longstanding and controversial that it has even inspired a word - balkanization - to describe the gradual breakup of a nation into smaller individual states.

Why did the alphabet only have 22 letters in the 1980s?

– Because E.T. went home and someone shot J.R!

ROUND 12

TURNING 80

Time for the final round! And appropriately enough, this one is all about turning 80…

No matter how you are feeling about stepping into your - gulp! - ninth decade, these questions are all about the famous people and figures for whom being an octogenarian was no big deal.

From Oscar winners to music makers, see how you get on with this final inspiring round of questions about some of the most extraordinary 80-year-olds in history!

1. Which of these famous figures turned 80 in 2006?
    a. Jimmy Carter
    b. Queen Elizabeth II
    c. Betty White
    d. Burt Bacharach
2. Filmmaker Ridley Scott released *All the Money in the World* just weeks after turning

80 years old in 2017. Which fellow octogenarian was nominated for a Best Supporting Actor Oscar for his role in the film?

a. Christopher Plummer
b. Dustin Hoffman
c. Clint Eastwood
d. Warren Beatty

3. Which legendary singer released the acclaimed album *Duets: An American Classic* to celebrate their 80th birthday in 2006, winning the Grammy Award for Best Traditional Pop Vocal Album the following year?

a. Ray Charles
b. Tony Bennett
c. Dame Vera Lynn
d. Petula Clark

4. All these famous figures not only lived long past 80, but they also lived to be over 100

years old! Can you put them in chronological order, beginning with the person who was born first?

a. Olivia de Havilland
b. George Burns
c. Irving Berlin
d. Grandma Moses

5. In 2016, 86-year-old Buzz Aldrin became the oldest person in history to… what?

a. Summit Mount Blanc
b. Visit the wreck of the Titanic
c. Travel to the South Pole
d. Win a Nobel Prize

6. Who won the Grammy for Best Folk Album at the 2024 Awards at the age of 80?

a. Bob Dylan
b. Joni Mitchell
c. Joan Baez
d. Judy Collins

7. In 2023, the director of *Killers of the Flower Moon* became the oldest person in movie history to be nominated for the Best Director Oscar, at the age of 81. The previous record holder had been the 79-year-old director of *Prizzi's Honor*.

   Name both directors for a point each.

8. Who am I?

   I am a legendary English actor, born in London in 1904. Having enrolled in drama school at the age of 17, I made my West End debut playing Romeo in 1924.

   By the following decade, I was already one of the London stage's most successful and well-respected stars and directed my first West End production in 1932 at the age of just 28.

   By the 1950s, I had made the move to films, and starred in my first Hollywood movie - an adaptation of Shakespeare's *Julius Caesar*

- opposite Marlon Brando in 1953; in the same year, I received a knighthood.

Over the next four decades, I continued to work on the stage, screen, radio, and television, winning countless awards for my performances.

In 1991, at the age of 87, I became the oldest person in history to win the coveted EGOT quartet of prizes, when - on top of my 1980 spoken word Grammy, 1982 Academy Award, and two Tony Awards - I received the Outstanding Lead Actor Emmy for my role in the drama *Summer's Lease*.

I died in 2000, at the age of 96. One of London's most illustrious and beautiful theaters is now named in my honor.

9. In 2013, a touring production of the play *Driving Miss Daisy* was launched, starring two legendary performers.

One - who was aged 88 at the time - was a five-time Tony Award-winning actress, who had also been nominated for a record 18 Emmys. The other - who was aged 82 - was a three-time Tony honoree, whose movie credits include *The Lion King* and *Star Wars*. Name both stars for a point each.

10. Which of the original stars of the 1961 movie *West Side Story* - who won an Oscar for their performance - also appeared in Steven Spielberg's 2021 remake at the age of 89?

    a. Marni Nixon
    b. Russ Tamblyn
    c. Richard Beymer
    d. Rita Moreno

11. In what year of his presidency did Joe Biden celebrate his 80th birthday?

    a. 2021
    b. 2022
    c. 2023

d. 2024

12. Mel Brooks was 88 years old when, in 2014, he was asked to leave his handprints in the concrete outside the famous Chinese Theatre on the Hollywood Walk of Fame. But what is unusual about his monument?

    a. He misspelled his name
    b. His name is written upside down
    c. His handprints have 11 fingers
    d. He wore woolen mittens

13. True or False? No one over the age of 80 has ever won a Nobel Prize.

14. Who won their second Academy Award for their performance in *The Father* in 2021, becoming the oldest Oscar-winning actor in history in the process?

    a. Anthony Hopkins
    b. Dustin Hoffman
    c. Vanessa Redgrave
    d. Julie Christie

15. Known for his deadpan humor and dry delivery, which American actor and comic was nominated for his sixth Emmy award in 2009 at the age of 80 - and won his first four years later for a guest role in the sitcom *The Big Bang Theory*?

SOLUTIONS

1. B. Queen Elizabeth II. The former queen was born on April 21, 1926.
2. A. Christopher Plummer. Plummer was 88 years old at the time, making him the oldest Oscar-nominated actor in movie history.
3. B. Tony Bennett.
4. D. Grandma Moses (1860), C. Irving Berlin (1888), B. George Burns (1896), A. Olivia de Havilland (1916)
5. C. Travel to the South Pole. Aldrin had earlier visited the North Pole in 1998.
6. B. Joni Mitchell. The award was Mitchell's eleventh.
7. Martin Scorsese and John Huston.
8. Sir John Gielgud.
9. Angela Lansbury and James Earl Jones.

10. D. Rita Moreno. Moreno also served as an executive producer on the 2021 movie.
11. B. 2022. Biden was born on November 20, 1942.
12. C. His handprints have 11 fingers. In typical comic style, Brooks wore a fake prosthetic finger when he added his handprints to the concrete, so his left hand has six digits!
13. False. In fact, there have been dozens of Nobel laureates aged 80-plus, including the authors Doris Lessing (who was 88 when she won the Nobel for Literature in 2007) and Alice Munro (who was 82 when she won the same prize in 2013). The oldest Nobel honoree of all time, meanwhile, is the American scientist John B Goodenough, who was 97 when he was awarded the Nobel Prize in Chemistry in 2019.
14. A. Anthony Hopkins.
15. Bob Newhart.

DID YOU KNOW?

- As well as being one of Hollywood's greatest-ever stars, Al Pacino is also recognized as one of the world's oldest fathers: he had his fourth child, a son named Roman, in 2023 at the age of 83!
- In 1980, to celebrate the birthday of Elizabeth, the Queen Mother - mother of Queen Elizabeth II, and the widow of King George VI - the British Royal Mint produced a unique silver 25 pence coin, or "crown."
- In 2016, legendary English actress Dame Sheila Hancock took on a role in the movie *Edie* about a widow who overcomes her husband's death by climbing one of the highest mountains in Scotland. To make the movie as realistic as possible, Hancock - at the age of 83 - completed the trek up the mountain herself!

- In 2013, Japanese mountaineer Yūichirō Miura became the oldest person in history to climb Mount Everest, just a few months shy of his 81st birthday!
- The oldest person to complete a marathon is Fauja Singh, who completed the Toronto Marathon in 2003 at the age of 92, in a time of five hours and 40 minutes. No mean feat considering that he only started marathon running as a hobby when he was 89!

By the time you're 80 years old, you've already learned everything. You only have to remember it.

– Bill Vaughan

CONCLUSION

And with that final round of inspirational quiz questions, your trivia challenge is complete!

So, how did you do? Could you correctly recall back to the 40s, 50s, and 60s to figure out the answers here? Could you remember the where's, who's, and what's of the past?

We hope you have enjoyed the challenge these past 100 or so pages have thrown at you - but don't be too dismayed if you lost a point here or there or had to resort to checking a couple of the answers. This was a rather fiendish challenge after all!

But now this challenge is complete, how about another? Maybe those last few facts and questions have given you some new ideas and it's time to set your sights on something new?

Are you now thinking of running your first marathon in the next eight or nine years?

Made in United States
Cleveland, OH
26 August 2025

19791705R00085